Cello Exam Pieces

ABRSM Grade 1
Selected from the 2020–2023 syllabus

Piano accompaniment

Contents

Cello consultant: Anita Strevens
Footnotes: Anthony Burton

Editorial guidance

We have taken the pieces in this book from a variety of sources. Where appropriate, we have edited the pieces to help you prepare for your performance. We have added metronome markings (in square brackets) and ornament realisations. The fingering and bowing indications have been amended where necessary to ensure a consistent approach within the album. Details of other changes or suggestions are given in the footnotes. Fingering, bowing and editorial additions are for guidance only: you do not have to follow them in the exam.

First published in 2019 by ABRSM (Publishing) Ltd,
a wholly owned subsidiary of ABRSM, 4 London Wall Place,
London EC2Y 5AU, United Kingdom
© 2019 by The Associated Board of the Royal Schools of Music
Distributed worldwide by Oxford University Press

Music origination by Julia Bovee
Cover by Kate Benjamin & Andy Potts, with thanks to Brighton College
Printed in England by Page Bros (Norwich) Ltd, on materials from
sustainable sources.

Mattachins

from *Orchesographie*

Arranged by Edward Huws Jones

Thoinot Arbeau
(1520–95)

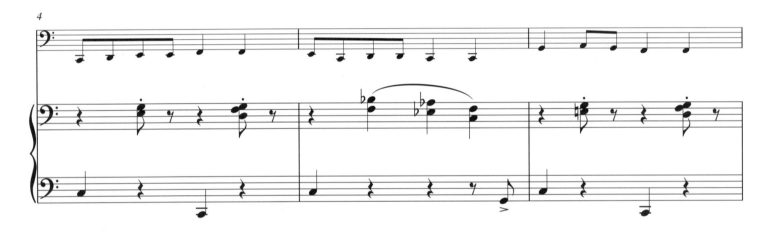

The melody of 'Mattachins' is from Thoinot Arbeau's *Orchesographie*, an instruction book for dancers published in Paris in 1589. The title indicates an old Italian dance performed with swords.

Adapted for Cello by ABRSM from *Violin Exam Pieces 2012–2015*, Grade 1 (ABRSM)

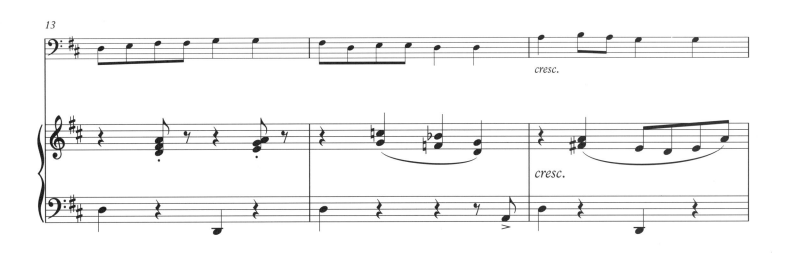

What is it all?

from *Third Booke of Ayres*

Arranged by Catherine Black
and Paul Harris

Thomas Campion
(1567–1620)

Thomas Campion was one of the leading composers of ayres in early 17th-century England. These are songs accompanied by a lute (a forerunner of the guitar). Unusually for the time, he wrote the words of his songs as well as the music. This song was published in 1617 in Campion's *Third Booke of Ayres*. Its first line asks the question: 'What is it all that men possess, among themselves conversing?'

© 1996 by The Associated Board of the Royal Schools of Music
Reproduced from *Time Pieces for Cello*, Volume 1, arranged by Catherine Black and Paul Harris (ABRSM)

John Ryan's Polka

Arranged by Edward Huws Jones

Trad. Irish

The polka is a lively dance which had its origins in the 19th century in Bohemia (part of the present-day Czech Republic). It quickly became popular in many other countries, including Ireland. 'John Ryan's Polka' is a well-known Irish dance tune for the fiddle. It may have been composed, or made popular, by the fiddler Seán Ryan of Nenagh in County Tipperary ('Seán' is the Irish equivalent of the name 'John'). The tune was heard on the soundtrack of the 1997 film *Titanic*.

© 2019 by The Associated Board of the Royal Schools of Music
Adapted for Cello by ABRSM from Edward Huws Jones: *Violin Star 2* (ABRSM)

B:1

Edelweiss

from The Sound of Music

Arranged by Alan Bullard

Music by Richard Rodgers (1902–79)
Lyrics by Oscar Hammerstein II (1895–1960)

The Sound of Music was the last musical written by the celebrated partnership of the composer Richard Rodgers and the lyricist Oscar Hammerstein II. It opened on Broadway in New York in November 1959 and ran for more than three and a half years; in 1965 it also became a very successful film. It is based on a real-life episode shortly before the Second World War, the escape from Nazi-occupied Austria of a family performing group, the Trapp Family Singers. 'Edelweiss' is a song sung in the group's last concert in Austria by the head of the family, Captain von Trapp. An edelweiss is a white Alpine flower, which for the Captain is a symbol of his beloved homeland.

Wiegenlied

D. 498

Arranged by David Blackwell

Franz Schubert
(1797–1828)

B:2

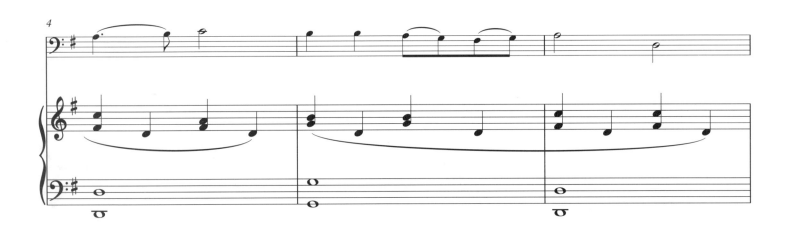

The Austrian composer Franz Schubert was one of the first important composers of *Lieder*, songs for voice and piano. Altogether he wrote over 600 of them. His well-known 'Wiegenlied' dates from November 1816, shortly before his 20th birthday. An English translation of the words, by an unknown author, begins: 'Sleep, sleep, you lovely sweet boy, your mother's hand rocks you gently.'

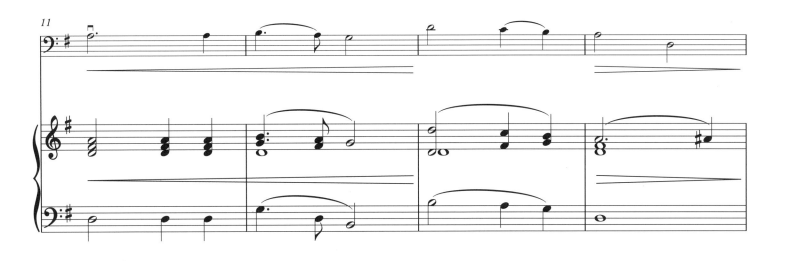

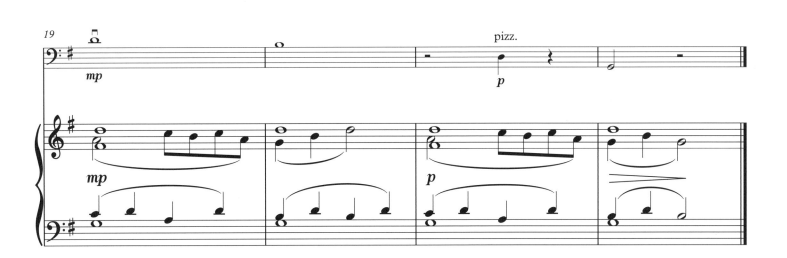

B:3

Star of the County Down

Arranged by Alan Bullard

Trad. Irish

'Star of the County Down' is an Irish folk melody, in the Aeolian mode. It is known by the words fitted to it by the writer Cathal McGarvey. These tell the story of a young man who catches sight of a pretty girl in Banbridge, in Northern Ireland, who he discovers is Rosie McCann, the 'star of the County Down', and immediately falls in love with her. The words of the refrain, beginning at the upbeat to bar 11, are:

From Bantry Bay down to Derry Quay,
And from Galway to Dublin town,
No maid I've seen like the brown colleen [brown-haired girl]
That I met in the County Down.

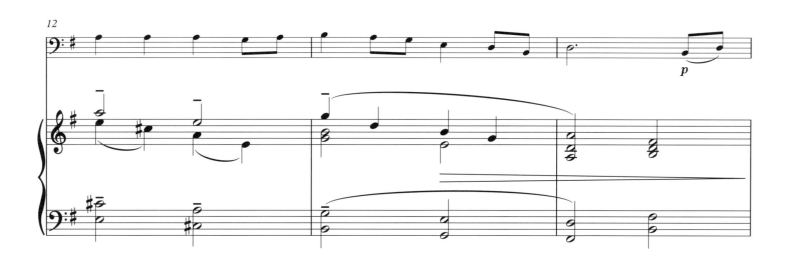

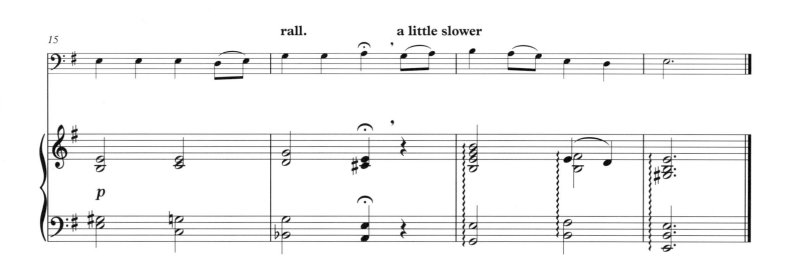

C:1

March

No. 1 from *Northern Skies*

James MacMillan
(born 1959)

Sir James MacMillan is a Scottish composer whose works have been performed by many of the world's leading orchestras and at many international festivals. His *Northern Skies* is a suite of seven pieces for cello and piano, written with young cellists in mind. It was commissioned by the cellist and teacher Myra Chahin, and first performed in the Scottish city of Glasgow in March 2001 by a group of four student cellists aged from 10 to 16. The suite begins with this brisk, resolute March.

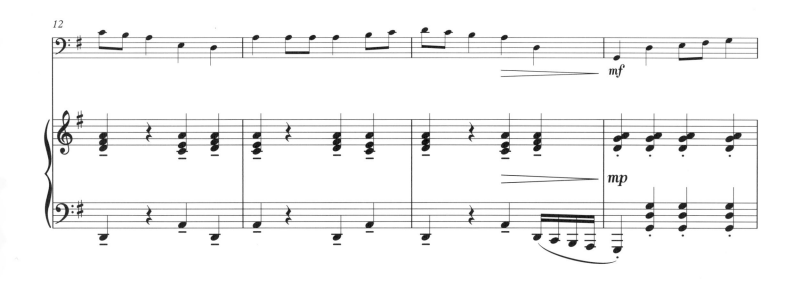

Flag Dance

Sheila M. Nelson
(born 1936)

Sheila M. Nelson is a former orchestral musician who is now best known as a teacher of violin and viola, and the author of many publications for young string players. This lively dance comes from her first graded collection, called *Piece by Piece*. A flag dance is a group dance involving the shaking, waving and spinning of coloured flags.

© Copyright 1992 by Boosey & Hawkes Music Publishers Ltd
Reproduced from *Piece by Piece 1* by permission of Boosey & Hawkes Music Publishers Ltd.

Turkey in the Straw

Arranged by David Blackwell

Trad. American

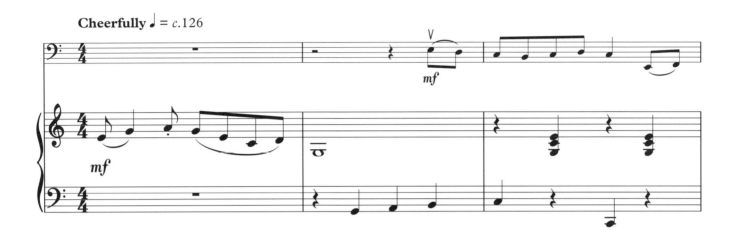

'Turkey in the Straw' is a traditional American fiddle tune played for dancing. It may be derived from the melody of an Irish ballad called 'The Old Rose Tree'. The tune has had various song texts fitted to it, and it was made popular as a song by minstrel shows in the 1820s and 1830s.

Cello Exam Pieces

ABRSM Grade 1

Selected from the 2020–2023 syllabus

Name

Date of exam

Contents

Cello consultant: Anita Strevens
Footnotes: Anthony Burton

Other pieces for Grade 1   DUET *with cello accompaniment*   PF/VC *with piano or cello accompaniment*

First published in 2019 by ABRSM (Publishing) Ltd,
a wholly owned subsidiary of ABRSM, 4 London Wall Place,
London EC2Y 5AU, United Kingdom
© 2019 by The Associated Board of the Royal Schools of Music
Distributed worldwide by Oxford University Press

Music origination by Julia Bovee
Cover by Kate Benjamin & Andy Potts, with thanks to Brighton College
Printed in England by Page Bros (Norwich) Ltd, on materials from
sustainable sources.

Mattachins

from *Orchesographie*

Arranged by Edward Huws Jones

Thoinot Arbeau
(1520–95)

Boisterous ♩ = *c*.88

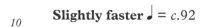

Slightly faster ♩ = *c*.92

The melody of 'Mattachins' is from Thoinot Arbeau's *Orchesographie*, an instruction book for dancers published in Paris in 1589. The title indicates an old Italian dance performed with swords.

What is it all?

from *Third Booke of Ayres*

A:2

Arranged by Catherine Black
and Paul Harris

Thomas Campion
(1567–1620)

Thomas Campion was one of the leading composers of ayres in early 17th-century England. These are songs accompanied by a lute (a forerunner of the guitar). Unusually for the time, he wrote the words of his songs as well as the music. This song was published in 1617 in Campion's *Third Booke of Ayres*. Its first line asks the question: 'What is it all that men possess, among themselves conversing?'

© 1996 by The Associated Board of the Royal Schools of Music
Reproduced from *Time Pieces for Cello*, Volume 1, arranged by Catherine Black and Paul Harris (ABRSM)

John Ryan's Polka

Arranged by Edward Huws Jones

Trad. Irish

The polka is a lively dance which had its origins in the 19th century in Bohemia (part of the present-day Czech Republic). It quickly became popular in many other countries, including Ireland. 'John Ryan's Polka' is a well-known Irish dance tune for the fiddle. It may have been composed, or made popular, by the fiddler Seán Ryan of Nenagh in County Tipperary ('Seán' is the Irish equivalent of the name 'John'). The tune was heard on the soundtrack of the 1997 film *Titanic*.

Edelweiss

from *The Sound of Music*

B:1

Arranged by Alan Bullard

Music by Richard Rodgers (1902-79)
Lyrics by Oscar Hammerstein II (1895-1960)

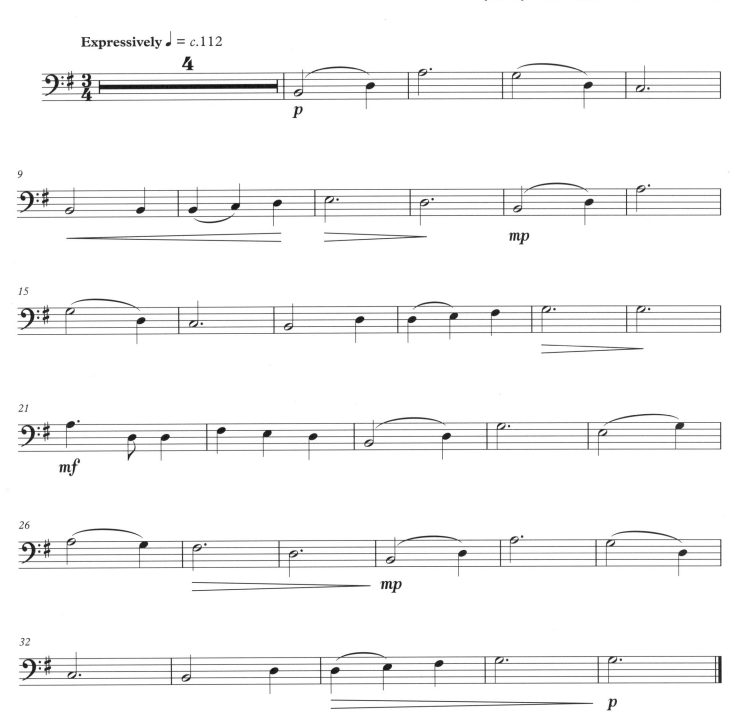

The Sound of Music was the last musical written by the celebrated partnership of the composer Richard Rodgers and the lyricist Oscar Hammerstein II. It opened on Broadway in New York in November 1959 and ran for more than three and a half years; in 1965 it also became a very successful film. It is based on a real-life episode shortly before the Second World War, the escape from Nazi-occupied Austria of a family performing group, the Trapp Family Singers. 'Edelweiss' is a song sung in the group's last concert in Austria by the head of the family, Captain von Trapp. An edelweiss is a white Alpine flower, which for the Captain is a symbol of his beloved homeland.

Wiegenlied

D. 498

B:2

Arranged by David Blackwell

Franz Schubert
(1797–1828)

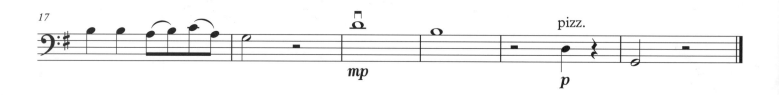

The Austrian composer Franz Schubert was one of the first important composers of *Lieder*, songs for voice and piano. Altogether he wrote over 600 of them. His well-known 'Wiegenlied' dates from November 1816, shortly before his 20th birthday. An English translation of the words, by an unknown author, begins: 'Sleep, sleep, you lovely sweet boy, your mother's hand rocks you gently.'

Star of the County Down

B:3

Arranged by Alan Bullard

Trad. Irish

'Star of the County Down' is an Irish folk melody, in the Aeolian mode. It is known by the words fitted to it by the writer Cathal McGarvey. These tell the story of a young man who catches sight of a pretty girl in Banbridge, in Northern Ireland, who he discovers is Rosie McCann, the 'star of the County Down', and immediately falls in love with her. The words of the refrain, beginning at the upbeat to bar 11, are:

From Bantry Bay down to Derry Quay,
And from Galway to Dublin town,
No maid I've seen like the brown colleen [brown-haired girl]
That I met in the County Down.

C♭ = Lift bow around.

C:1

March

No. 1 from *Northern Skies*

James MacMillan
(born 1959)

Sir James MacMillan is a Scottish composer whose works have been performed by many of the world's leading orchestras and at many international festivals. His *Northern Skies* is a suite of seven pieces for cello and piano, written with young cellists in mind. It was commissioned by the cellist and teacher Myra Chahin, and first performed in the Scottish city of Glasgow in March 2001 by a group of four student cellists aged from 10 to 16. The suite begins with this brisk, resolute March.

Flag Dance

Sheila M. Nelson
(born 1936)

Sheila M. Nelson is a former orchestral musician who is now best known as a teacher of violin and viola, and the author of many publications for young string players. This lively dance comes from her first graded collection, called *Piece by Piece*. A flag dance is a group dance involving the shaking, waving and spinning of coloured flags.

C:3

Turkey in the Straw

Arranged by David Blackwell

Trad. American

'Turkey in the Straw' is a traditional American fiddle tune played for dancing. It may be derived from the melody of an Irish ballad called 'The Old Rose Tree'. The tune has had various song texts fitted to it, and it was made popular as a song by minstrel shows in the 1820s and 1830s.